10 SIMPLE WAYS TO FIND HAPPINESS

Giuseppe Moschella

Table of Contents

HOW IT
ALL BEGAN

I t was October 2021,
right after closing a production show in the main
theater on board a major cruise line,
where, I was working as a Cruise Director/Entertainment
Director at the time,
I was walking backstage while the crowd cheered, and
gave a final look to the audience where I saw
a gentleman around his 50s. He was standing up close to
the stage. He had called my name.

My play-out was on. The atmosphere was great. I did not
want this man to ruin the moment.
He did not seem like a threat though, so I decided to stop,
go down the stairs and speak to him.
I was not sure whether it was a good decision.
The guy could have punched me in the face for the last
joke I said.
He was way bigger than me, and after all, I am a very
small Italian man.

The guy named Joe was wearing glasses, had grayish hair, was quite large and utterly surprised by the fact that I actually came to meet him. He thought I would have just ignored him.

While I was surprised I did not fall down the stairs. I'm well-known for being kinda goofy.

He called me Giovanni, although my name is Giuseppe, but it did not matter.

That's when, he posed a question that got me thinking:

"How come you are always genuinely happy? What do you do to always be so positive?

What drugs do you take?"

I wanted to throw a few jokes and leave, but then I noticed that he was being serious.

He was waiting for "the answer" that could make his quest of happiness easier.

He suffered from depression. Joe shared with me that he often thought about committing suicide.

He came on this cruise vacation to find some sort of joy in life he seemed to have lost forever.

Joe was insecure, curious and also very kind. He was asking for help.

My mamma taught me to always help someone in need with all resources I have, and never to ignore someone in pain because tomorrow, the one in pain could be me.

What was I going to answer to this man? There's no secret. There is no key to happiness.
It's not like in The Chronicles of Narnia where you open a door, and you encounter mythical creatures and then... there's happiness sitting there, arms crossed waiting for you to show up.
He caught me very unprepared. I told him to wait. I would find him again. Why was I always happy?

That night, I went to the top deck. The sky was beautiful. The waves brought peace and calm to my soul. The ship radiated so much power and positivity. My mind was clear.
I kept staring at the ocean when suddenly "EUREKA". I felt like my fellow Sicilian Archimedes.

I would prepare a talk. A presentation about happiness.
I thought, "maybe I should write down the top 10 things I do to be happy".
And so I started writing "10 Simple Ways To Find Happiness".

It took me 2 hours and 48 minutes. I remember that exactly because I played a 3 hours long playlist and I had

12 minutes left to chill, unwind and enjoy those last tracks.

The last song was Wicked Game by Chris Isaak. I sang it so happily loudly. I did not give a damn.

The morning after, I met Joe and his wife at a lovely Italian café on board.

I was having an espresso when he walked by. I stopped him and with great excitement (I'm famous for being overly excited) I told him I had created something special for him.

Not only that, but I was also going to present it the next day. He was astonished by the news and gave me a hug while whispering the words "Thank you". His wife was rather surprised, as she did not believe I would take the time to do this, perhaps I was just going to disappear.

That day, I entered the room at 9:53am. The talk started at 10:15am. There was no one in sight.

I was slightly disappointed and told my colleague to call me later. I needed a coffee. Maybe two.

While I was chatting to people and looking at the waves outside the window, my phone rang.

My assistant informed me that they were going to add extra chairs as the room was full.

I thought it was a joke and I took my time to get to the place. I am Italian. We are elegantly late.

When I finally entered, the room was packed, but I could not find Joe.

I was about to start, but wanted to wait an extra second to see if he showed up.

I looked to the left and there he was... I was ready to begin.

That day, I hosted the most interesting talk I have ever hosted.

I had a plan in mind, a line to follow. I improvised most of it as I could really feel this presentation.

This was not just another talk. This was different. It had the purpose of making someone happy.

I remember stuttering halfway through. Not only because I could not find the words, but also because I took a moment to actually look at everyone in the audience.

They were laughing, cheering. They were happy and so was I.

I spoke to several people at the end of it. Some thanked me. Some gave the biggest hugs.

Others shook my hand. Many left without saying a word. Joe was waiting his turn.

He then gave me the longest hug, handed me a piece of paper and left without saying a word.

It said:

Thank you!
I am ready to be happy now...

1.

Wake up!

The secret is in the morning

No more snooze buttons. Do not postpone your day!

As you read this page, so many people are snoozing, delaying and turning off those alarms.

Don't be those people!

How many times do we tell ourselves:

"I am going to wake up in 5 minutes. Maybe 10 or 15. I'll skip breakfast and sleep in. I am so tired."

And then leave with a frown, and we rush through our morning. We rush through our life.

In conclusion, we are late for work, late for school, we are late for our life to begin.

Although, we always manage to find time to check notifications... that post was quite funny.

Don't be late! Take action. Get up. Come alive! Your day won't start without you.

Postponing your awakening is going to affect your morale for the entire day.

The more you postpone that alarm. The more you postpone your happiness.

So, rise-and-shine at the first alarm. Make sure your alarm is LOUD. Your phone is far away,

So you have to stand up to stop it, and since you're already standing, why not start your day?

Use a song you like or hate. I usually sing that tune for the first 2-3 minutes of my day.

Singing stimulates multiple areas of the brain at the same time. We want that brain to get-going.

And if you suck as a singer, for sure your brain will wake up to stop you from doing it.

The first step to a great morning is making the first step "out of bed". Easy. Simple. No-sweat.

Once you accomplish that, you can make the next step, and then the next one. And more.

Brush your teeth, make some breakfast, open the windows, feel the air, take a deep breath.

Do whatever makes you feel alive. It is a new day. It is time to feel great. Powerful. Present.

Today is your day. It's no one else's. You decide who you are today. Choose your best version.

Some famous personalities recommend waking up at 5am.

I am not telling you to join the club. I am telling you to just wake up and open your eyes.

Some meditate, some exercise, some take a shower, some make delicious breakfasts.

Don't do what "some" do. Do what you would do to make your morning successful.

Navy Admiral William would tell you to make your bed. I would make good coffee. And you?

Rest days are great, but if you rest all day every day, then you will not have achieved anything by the time you reach "the ultimate resting time". Wake up! Open those eyes and your heart.

Cold showers may help. My "friend" used to do a shot of Tequila. That's not good. Or is it?

And when you do not want to wake up. That's when you have to! #GoodMorningSunshine

Waking up is like writing the first word of chapter "today".
Write the most inspiring words.
Fill that page with joy, enthusiasm, even fear.
Do not close that book called life and go back to sleep
when the world is waiting for you to grab that pen and
make today <u>exceptional.</u>

2.

Be present

Focus. Engage. Be There.
Look, Feel. Smell. Taste. Experience.

Be present in conversations. Live the moment. Don't disconnect. Your brain is not out of range. If you think about the next few hours...if you think about the future. You hit "skip" on the present.
You are not there for people when they talk to you or for yourself at the present moment.

So listen proactively. React. Think about the "right now". You are here now reading this book.
Enjoy this current line. Read it word by word. Don't skip to the end.

Don't check your phone constantly while reading. While "living".
Life is not short, it's quite long, but we make it shorter when we keep hitting on the skip button. When we don't enjoy the moment due to boredom, lack of enthusiasm, tiredness or impatience.

"Not being present" will negatively affect your day, your relationships and your happiness.

When you're eating. When you're drinking. When you're cooking.
Enjoy the food. Savor that beverage. Taste your cuisine.
The pace of our lives is increasing, and so is everything we do.
Truly experience the sensation of every bite of your day.

Do one thing at the time. We love multitasking. Multitasking is cool. Business people multitask.
But is it really cool? Is doing a thousand things at the same time and focusing on none very cool?
When we do too much simultaneously, we forget what we do. We are actually doing too little.

I remember once completing a series of tasks altogether.
I looked like a freak. Maybe I was.
I was done way before the deadline. However, I could not remember exactly what I had done.
Was it really that effective? I had finished, yes. But, I had not learned anything from it.

Also, be there for the people who need you.
If you are not there for the people who need you, then why are you even there?

We are often not even there for ourselves. Then, who are we there for?

Typically, we talk about what we are going to do tomorrow, and we forget what we can do today.
Why are you already thinking about the next day?
Enjoy the current one. There's so much we can do. Let your future self-think about tomorrow.
Your present self wants to have a hell of a good time right now. Are you ready?

To conclude, Mindfulness has always been the key to many people's success.
Be present. Be mindful. It will make you happy.

Live this very moment.
As you breathe, you read, you think, just smile.
Let your future self-think about tomorrow,
while you enjoy this awesome ride you are on <u>today.</u>

3.

Express Gratitude

Thank genuinely and sincerely.
Show appreciation. Say Grazie.

There is always something to be grateful for. Always someone to thank.

Thank your neighbor. Thank your friend, your lover, and never forget to thank yourself.

Find a moment during your day to write down what you are grateful for today. Say it out loud!

While I am writing this book, it's freezing cold outside, and I am grateful for the cozy couch I am sitting on, the warm socks I am wearing, the delicious green tea I am sipping and the smell of hot yummy margherita pizza cooking in the oven. I better check on it before it burns.

Appreciate life, value the little things, respect your friends, treasure the moments, cherish today.

Sometimes we forget to thank people after they went the extra mile for us.

We forgot to thank our parents when they came back home exhausted from work, and they had to cook for us, wash our clothes, motivate us, educate us, be a role model and take us places.

It's never too late to thank people. Be grateful. It will make them happy. It will make you happy.

Gratitude is associated with greater happiness. You want to feel more positive emotions,

then build stronger relationships, put a smile on someone's face. Gratitude is your answer.

Don't neglect the power you and other people may gain from it.

My grandma used to spit on her customer's minestrone if they did not say "thank you".

It costs you nothing and will make an impact on your day.

Now, let's try a game together. Close your eyes and for a few seconds...

Thank yourself, thank your closest friends, thank whoever you want to thank today. And mean it!

Don't just close your eyes and rush to the end of it. Do not forget what you learned.

You are now awake. You want to be present and express gratitude.

I am grateful for everything, and I am grateful for the fact that I woke up this morning.

Not everyone goes to sleep and wakes up the next day.

Today and every day, I am grateful for my grandfather. He taught me so much.

He always used to thank all his employees, friends, and his family. Even for the smallest things.

He always said "Grazie Mille" and taught me to say so.

Never forget to express gratitude.

A strong and real person knows how to thank.

My grandpa was the greatest man I've ever met.

Thank you, Nonno Giuseppe.

Gratitude is the strongest currency there is.
Its value is unlimited, and we should never forget to give it the
right importance.
A "thank you" costs you nothing, while it makes you richer.

4.

Bring music to your life

*Never underestimate the sublime
healing power of music.*

Music is extraordinary. Music is extremely powerful and beneficial to our lives. Silence is good. It helps us reflect. Music makes us create. Rejoice. Kindle passions. True hope.

Music is all around us. It's everywhere. We must embrace it. Welcome it. Open our hearts to it.

Let music enter your life. Hit play on the soundtrack of your day and pump up the volume.

Play it during your commute. Play music while you exercise.

Listen to a song while you cook. Always turn the car radio on.

Listen to a track while making love. Tender romantic tunes. Well, that depends on your desires.

LISTEN TO THE WORLD!
The world is the biggest and best orchestra conductor.

Everything around us makes a sound.

From the rain falling on the ground to the wind blowing.

From a phone vibrating to a baby laughing. Any sound is music.

Music accompanies us every day of our lives. We just have to open our ears and heart to it.

We, ourselves, are music when we talk, when we walk, when we breathe, and we sleep.

Music is crucial to our day and has considerable positive effects.

Music speaks to us and silences us.

It connects you to others. It is your best companion.

When you're feeling down, insecure. Anxiety is taking over you. You might feel unprepared for a challenge. That's when the right song will bring you back on track.

Let music surround you and guide you towards happiness.

Let it enchant your soul. It alleviates your pain and makes your brain healthier.

It can transport you to your happy place. Music is magnificent!

Now, imagine a world without music. A day without any sounds, any voices, any noise.

Would you like to live in a world like that?

Nietzsche would not be happy. Me neither. What about you?

Let's play another game!
Try reading this page once again, but this time play a song. Loud and clear. Blast it and experience it. Feel the sounds. The instruments. The beats. Embrace your emotions.
Let music improve your mood, make you more relaxed or hyped.
Music will enhance your reading experience; it will enhance your life experience.
Now. hit play!

Music keeps us alive.
Music makes everything alive.
And even when I die, I want to die listening to music.

5.

Celebrate every single victory

Life is to be celebrated every single day.

When we are kids, we look forward to each anniversary, birthday, ceremony, any occasion to celebrate. Celebrations make us happy, and we find joy in other people's celebrations.

When we grow older, we believe we are too old or too cool to throw a birthday party.

We are now too mature to celebrate our victories and anniversaries.

There's no reason to celebrate Valentine's Day, since we've been together for too long.

No time to celebrate Christmas this year. Too much work to do.

Why meeting friends and family for New Year's Eve? It's just another year!

No, my friend. Never let a special day go unnoticed. Celebrate LIFE!

Celebrate your birthday or the fact that you're still here.

You never know. Life happens, and sometimes life does not happen anymore.

Celebrate every victory, every moment, every gesture, every occasion.
The victories you celebrate are the ones you will remember.
Raise your glass, make a speech, hug your friends and thank everyone around you.

In Italy, we celebrate ANYTHING!
At the beginning, I thought it was just an excuse not to work.
We Italians are famous for just enjoying "la dolce vita", but we are also famous for being joyful, and full of life. If you do not know what to celebrate, come to Italy! We will find you something.

Celebrate your success and everyone else's success.
Do not complain about all things that went wrong.
Celebrate what went right.
Acknowledge and appreciate the win, and then? Move on to the next challenge!
Do not wait until you reach your final goal to celebrate.
Celebrate the small triumphs en route to the grand finale.
Remind yourself that you're successful and are on the right path.

Rome wasn't built in a day. It will take time for you to achieve your ultimate target.

Your final goal is composed of many tiny ones. Accomplish those and celebrate them first.

Applaud yourself, congratulate yourself! Reward yourself. Your reward could be anything: An iced latte. A good book. A movie. A big bowl of spaghetti.

Do not only celebrate victories. Celebrate people, celebrate friendships, celebrate love.

And you, what are you going to celebrate today?

I live my whole life as a huge celebration.
I toast, congratulate, cheer, laugh and pop another bottle.
Life's a show, a party, and I want to get the best tickets.

6.

Love

Someone. Something. Some places.
Some ideas. Fall in love with Life.

Love your morning. Your puppy. A stranger's perfume, the ocean, the bed you sleep in.

Fall in love with your day. If you are not in love with it, everything around you is dead.

The colors are dark, the path is obscure, everything is sad and boring.

Love will bring colors to your life. Love will make a good day a great day.

When you fall in love with people, with things. Everything moves, everything comes alive.

Love yourself, your friend, your partner and your home.

Today, more than ever before, you should love yourself and those around you.

We lost the value of love. The importance of it. We wait too long and then love too little.

Love and happiness are connected. If you want to be happy, then love every second of your day.

Fall in love with a song, a picture, a street and a name. When you're in love, the world lights up. Everything has a different shape and a better look.

Don't be afraid of being heartbroken. I'd be afraid to not fall in love. That's worse.

Say yes to love! Don't try to understand it. Go ahead and experience it.

Connect with other human beings. Connect with the world. Don't just connect to the Wi-Fi.

Love is a splendid thing. Make your life splendid.

Love brings warmth, brilliance and entertainment to your life.

Love is insanely powerful. It inspires you to grow. To go higher. Makes you feel secure.

It stimulates your brain, ignites your soul and opens your eyes.

It's not easy to love. It's not easy to let people love you. Nothing good in this life is easy, though.

Let love conquer your heart. Brighten your day and warm your house.

I fall in love a million times a day.

Today, I fell in love with the smell of fresh Parmesan when I opened my fridge.

I fell in love with the warm ginseng I drank while looking outside the window.

Fell in love with that blue blue sky and its immense clouds.

Watching a YouTube Video, I fell in love with Matthew McConaughey's smile at the Oscars.

And then, with Aretha Franklin's voice when singing "Mister Spain".

You are foolish not to love and even more foolish when you know you're in love, but choose to ignore it because you do not have time or are too afraid to admit it.

You are saying no to happiness by doing that. What is the time if you don't live well?

Tempus fugit, yes it does. Because we let it flee.

Love is miraculous. Believe in miracles. Believe in love.

Love is everything you want it to be, just make sure you let it be, and it will be.

7.

Complete tasks.

*When you do not complete it, the smallest
thing may get bigger and larger.
The task becomes an issue, a problem,
and it will make you unhappy.*

Finish what you started. Do not procrastinate. Your future self will hate you for that.

A day is composed of 24 hours. In 24 hours, we can do so many things.

We are exceptionally capable human beings. We can do so much in just a minute.

Do not leave something you can do now to later or tomorrow.

That little insignificant thing will join a cluster of many other small insignificant things, and that cluster will become bigger and taller to the point of burying you and weighing tons.

Those tons will turn into anxiety, stress and sadness. If you can't complete it at that precise moment, then promise yourself that you will complete it soon. AND COMPLETE IT!

There was a day, not long ago, when I felt sad and worthless. I felt like I could not do anything.

I was overwhelmed by little tasks I had postponed and never even started.

I had nightmares and would take hours to fall asleep. So many thoughts suppressed me.

I had the worst mornings and the most horrible nights. Then I told myself: Complete those tasks.

It took me a LONG time. I am not going to lie. I spent, what seemed to be an eternity, finalizing projects and starting some others. Drank liters of coffee and then finally finished.

I felt so relieved. So energetic and happy, even if I had missed sleep and lost track of time.

I put my shorts on, running shoes and headphones and went out jogging.

I was revitalized, rejuvenated, serene and worry-free.

All those demons that were chasing me for weeks had finally disappeared.

When I saw the sunrise, I realized a new day had just begun and what made me sad belonged to yesterday. Today is today. Looking forward to what's coming next.

Complete your tasks 1 by 1. Don't do what I did. I was desperate. Divide them into smaller tasks.

When working out, you don't do 30 reps in a row. You divide them by 3 or 4, right?

You are not going to learn an instrument, a subject or a skill overnight.

Dogecoin won't reach the moon right now. It takes time, but you have to start.

Baby steps make a baby move.

Are you ready to move now?

Tasks will be presented to you continuously throughout your day.

You have the time. You just need motivation.

I hope this page will motivate, inspire and push you to finish those uncompleted tasks.

If there's something that keeps bothering you. It upsets you. Then drop this book and complete it before it starts obsessing you. I will see you when you're done. I know you'll be back.

Completing a task is not an easy task.
Feeling happy after completing it. That is easy.

8.

Call your mama

Your dad. Your sibling. A friend.
A lover. Call them! Speak to them!

If you do not call them, they will stop calling you.
There will be a day in your life when you will have to call someone.
And you will have no one to call. You don't want to have a full directory and no one to call.

Today's technology allows us to communicate so easily and promptly.
Shoot a message. Record a 10-minute-long voice-note.
Send a picture. A selfie. A video.
Human beings are communicators. We love to talk, to interact, to exchange ideas.
Speak to other people, not only to yourself.
Share, listen, engage and value those never-ending phone calls with friends, lovers and family.
Never forget to say hi and goodbye.

Not long ago, in order to send a message to a friend, you had to drive to their house.

Sometimes, it was not even possible because you had to fly to see them.

Today, you are one click away.

During the pandemic, I was grateful for the ability to speak to friends.

I spent 27 days locked in a Miami hotel room by myself.

It was thanks to those annoying group chats, those poor-quality video calls and blurry selfies that I made myself happy every day. I could have ignored them and locked myself in my thoughts.

I chose to open those messages, answer those calls, and just talk.

There's a friend, a parent, someone you have wanted to call for a while, but you have not yet.

Take your phone. Go out for a walk. Make that phone call and speak to that person.

When she was only 17, my cousin called me and I did not want to answer.

I was "too busy" playing video games. I forgot to call her later.

I do not recall her last words. I do not remember when was the last time we spoke.

All I remember is that I did not take that call. She was gone the day after.

We spend minutes, if not hours checking the updates and new posts of a person we do not even know on social media. But yet... we have no time to call people we actually know.
If you don't have time, you can make the time.

The game we are playing has not stopped yet. Next level.
Grab that phone and dial someone's number. You know who you want to call.
I will see you later on the next page. I am keeping you busy today, eh?

I'd rather have 5 favorite numbers to call than 100
I'm not sure if I can call.

9.

Go out

Don't spend a full day at home.
Always find time to go out and experience.

During the last years, we have all spent so many days at home without being able to go out.
We have all ordered online because we could not go to the shop.

Looked outside the window, through the peephole, and dreamt about the outside world.

Life is not lived through a peephole, a phone or in a small dark room.

Get out of your bed. Out of your house. Take this book and walk around your neighborhood.

People might think you're crazy. Let them think that. Who cares?

You are not the first one and will not be the last one walking around with a book.

Please do not forget to watch the traffic when crossing the road.

I've seen people so immersed in a book to forget they were also immersed in the traffic of Milan.

Feel the wind blowing, inhale and exhale the outside air, feel the ground on your feet.
Let the sun hit your face, the birds fly over your head.
Look at the moon before heading to bed.

Smart working is convenient, efficient and profitable.
"Smart living" involves outside energy.
Go out and let that energy take you on a spectacular journey that is called life.
Make sure each day is also spent outside. Leave the office. The house. Feel the adrenaline.
Get another perspective. A different angle. Turn your perspective upside down.
Your ideas may flourish, your happiness will increase, so will calmness and peace within.

Get a boost of vitamin D. Walk with no direction in mind.
Find green areas in your city and feel nature. You will only gain from it.
I love reading/listening to music under a tree. Next to a river or close to the shore by the local beach.
It's very dramatic and makes me feel like I am on the cover of some magazine.
Maybe I am just dumb, but I love it, and it cheers me up.

Have you tried to leave all your belongings at home and leave (But don't forget the keys)?

During a sad time in my life, I was only working from home and even forgot how the outside world looked. Then one day, I started waking up at 6am to run to the beach and watch the sunrise. That little gesture changed my mood completely. That probably saved me from despair.

The world is yours to take, to explore and adventure.

Go on a holiday. Travel. Visit. Ride a bike in the wind. Exercise outdoors.

Never let a day end, without a breath of fresh air. Enjoy your time away from the daily grind.

When you're stuck. You can't find a solution to that problem, go find it outside.

Where are you right now? I hope you find yourself somewhere nice outside. Finishing this page.

*It is inside yourself and outside in the world
that you may find the most interesting answers
to the hardest questions.
The most glorious minutes to the saddest minutes.
The most inspirational thoughts to those lazy days.
The brightest light to the darkest nights.*

10.

Express yourself

Feel good and happy with yourself.

D on't be intimidated by yourself. You know who you are. Find the courage to tell others.

If you can't find yourself in the position you are in, then change position.

Look at it from a different angle, look at yourself in a different mirror.

Some people go to Europe on a trip to find themselves –

or at least that's the excuse I told my parents when I first went to visit Amsterdam.

Find yourself and express it to others, but especially express it for your own self.

You want to feel good about yourself. Appreciated. Genuinely comfortable and not fake.

Do not wear a mask. Don't hide behind someone or something.

There's nothing better than feeling how you want to, and nothing worse than pretending.

Never feel uncomfortable with who you truly are. Have faith in yourself!

I met many people in my life who often stayed quiet and did not share their opinions for the fear of being rejected or terrorized by someone's opinion.

Everyone will always have an opinion, but the most valuable opinion is the one you have about yourself. If you believe in who you are and are ready to throw that mask away and prove yourself, then I wish you the best of luck. The grandest joy. The happiest days.

Find courage. Be brave. Bold. Authentic.

Expressing yourself goes on many levels, many faces, a huge array of aspects and meanings.

Today, I encourage you to do so. Do not act differently, pretend to be someone else to fit in.

If you, as you truly are, do not fit in, then that place is not for you.

Luca loved classical music, but he never told anyone cuz the cool kids listened to Death Metal.

He became a brilliant pianist. The cool kids, now adults, bought tickets to his performance.

Francesca adored Die Hard yet always watched it alone. Girls were into Gossip Girl.

Her husband and her watch Die Hard together all the time.

Marco had a crush on Stefano. He was scared. Pisa was a small city. Not that open-minded.
Today they are happily married. Their love and joy for life inspired many others to come out.

And you, who are you?
Final game, my friend...
Put both hands on this page, close your eyes and visualize yourself today and yourself in 10 years. Where do you want to be? Who do you truly want to be? This new game starts now.

Yell your name!
Let the world know who you truly are.
It is in the affirmation of yourself that you
will find your true being.
You are wonderful!
Do not let anyone tell you differently.

HOW IT ALL CONTINUES

Thank you for taking time to read this book.

For dedicating time to yourself.

For opening yourself to new visions.

For allowing me to enter your life, even for just a tiny moment.

The intent of this book is not finding instant happiness.

With this book, I want the reader to find a line that will enlighten the day.

A sparkle in the darkness.

A butterfly in a polluted city.

A slice of hope when no one believes in you.

A page to assist through the day and get you back on track when you're off the path.

Happiness is real and can be found.

Seek for it, adventure yourself, feel good.

I have encountered many happy people and shared many happy moments. I am grateful for that.

Happiness. Felicidad. Bonheur. Fericire. Szczęście. Felicità. Glueck.
It always sounds nice. Even in German.

Read this book at different stages of your life.
In different environments. Different seasons.
Read the book upside down.
Play those little games and never give up.
Even when everything is falling apart. Even when you're on the verge of breaking down.
Get up, stand up, wake up!

Enjoy life, cherish every single moment.
I hope you found at least one reason to live a better life today.

Thank you, Joe, for allowing me to help you.
I hope that this book will help many others who are not feeling ok right now.
Many others who are looking for motivation to become greater and stronger.
I truly hope the talk I presented on that cruise ship really made you feel happy.

This goes beyond the "10".

However, making others feel happy makes me feel happy too.

May happiness prevail in your life.

ABOUT THE AUTHOR

Giuseppe Moschella is a world traveler, a life-lover, a passion seeker, a crazy outsider, a quiet reader, a terrible singer, a wonderful friend and a happy eccentric lunatic.

Born and raised in the stunning summer paradise Taormina, Sicily - Italy. Giuseppe was born the 4th of August 1993, 2 years after his idol Freddie Mercury passed away.

He's a stubborn Leo that developed an affinity for travel and adventure at a young age.
He has even explored all 7 continents - twice!
After living in several countries and partied in many more, he now speaks six languages and has a degree in

Languages and Communication from the Universities of Catania, Italy
and Potsdam, Germany. Berlin will always be his favorite city.

He is passionate about music, entertainment, fitness and good people with a good smile.

Follow his crazy adventures on Instagram @thathappyitalian

Printed in Great Britain
by Amazon

36359601R00031